A Fairy-Tale Life

A Fairy-Tale Life

A Story about Hans Christian Andersen

by Joann Johansen Burch

illustrations by Liz Monson

A Carolrhoda Creative Minds Book

Carolrhoda Books, Inc./Minneapolis

To my grandmother, Marie Olson, who was proud to have grown up in Hans Christian Andersen's Odense, and my grandfather, Carl Olsen. To my aunt, Grethe Johansen, my uncle and aunt, Max and Mona Johansen, and my cousins, Anne Mette, Ingelise, and Bent. To my cousin, Else Johansen Schultz, and her children, Annette, Birgitte, and Jesper. To my cousins, Brita and Jørgen Thorsted, who live in Odense, and their children, Anne Charlotte and Christina.—JJB

Editor's Note: Liz Monson created the original artwork for this book using a mixture of painting and paper cutting. Cutting fanciful figures from paper was one of Hans Christian Andersen's favorite pastimes and is still popular in Denmark today.

This book is available in two editions:
Library binding by Carolrhoda Books, Inc.,
    a division of Lerner Publishing Group
Soft cover by First Avenue Editions,
    an imprint of Lerner Publishing Group
241 First Avenue North
Minneapolis, MN 55401 U.S.A.

Website address: www.lernerbooks.com

Library of Congress Cataloging-in-Publication Data

Burch, Joann Johansen.
    A fairy-tale life : a story about Hans Christian Andersen / Joann
Johansen Burch ; illustrations by Liz Monson.
        p.   cm. — (A Carolrhoda creative minds book)
    Includes bibliographical references.
    ISBN 0-87614-829-1 (lib. bdg. : alk. paper)
    ISBN 0-87614-642-6 (pbk. : alk. paper)
    1. Andersen, H. C. (Hans Christian), 1805–1875—Biography—Juvenile
literature. 2. Authors, Danish—19th century—Biography—Juvenile
literature. [1. Andersen, H. C. (Hans Christian), 1805–1875. 2. Authors,
Danish.] I. Monson, Liz, ill. II. Title. III. Series.
PT8119.B78   1994
839.8'136—dc20   93-48463

Manufactured in the United States of America
2 3 4 5 6 7 – MA – 06 05 04 03 02 01

Table of Contents

① The Shoemaker's Son

Hans Christian raced down the street, trying to escape the neighborhood boys. He stumbled over the rough cobblestones, and the boys nearly caught him. But his legs were longer than theirs. With a quick glance over his shoulder, he scrambled frantically up a tree in the churchyard. While he held his breath, the boys ran right past him.

At last he was safe. Safe from the boys who played too rough for him and took such delight in making him cry. Safe from those who called him "stork legs" because he was so tall and thin. And safe, for the moment at least, from the others who said he looked like a scarecrow with his mop of white-blond hair, tiny eyes, big nose, and huge hands and feet.

When Hans Christian thought it was safe to come down, he found he was stuck in the tree. No matter how hard he tried, he couldn't untangle his long arms and legs. Fortunately, one of the neighborhood girls saw him and hurried to tell Hans Christian's father. (And fortunately, none of the neighborhood boys were around to make fun of him, trapped in a tree.)

Hans Andersen soon came to rescue his son, but he didn't scold the boy. Hans and his wife, Anne Marie, tried to protect their son from the bullies who were always picking on him. He was their only child, and they showered him with love and attention. So did his grandmother. Hans Christian was her pride and delight, and she visited him daily.

The Andersens lived in Odense, a small town on the island of Fyn in Denmark, where Hans Christian was born on April 2, 1805. In those days, the world had no electric lights, telephones, cars, or radios. Odense had a castle, however, where the Danish crown prince made his home. Hans Christian always liked living in a town with a real castle and a real prince. He was certain he would live in a castle himself one day.

For the time being, Hans Christian and his family shared a small house with two other families on one of the poorest streets in town. They had only one room with a tiny kitchen at the back. Hans Andersen was a shoemaker, and his workbench, a big bed, and a chest of drawers took up most of the space. Hans Christian's small cot was stored under his parents' bed during the day so there would be enough room to walk around.

The place was cheery, with jars of flowers on the windowsills and snow-white curtains around the two windows. Painted landscapes decorated the door panels. On the walls were colorful pictures, including a portrait of Napoléon, who was the French emperor and Hans Andersen's hero.

A ladder in the kitchen led up to the roof, where Anne Marie had a tiny garden. She grew vegetables in a box placed in the gutter between the peaked roof of their house and the one next door. Hans Christian liked to climb up to the roof garden and watch what was going on in the town below. He felt as safe and secure as he would if he were a king in a castle. Hans Christian loved his rooftop hideaway, but sometimes he felt lonely there. He didn't have friends his age.

Before he was old enough for school, Anne Marie often took her son down to the Odense River where she worked washing other people's clothes.

Hans Christian played happily by himself along the banks. Sometimes he sang to a Chinese prince who lived beneath the water's surface. (One of the washerwomen had told Hans Christian that China was on the other side of the world, right under the Odense River, and he believed her!) He daydreamed about the prince coming out of the river and taking him back to live in his kingdom in China.

China, he reasoned, would be a fairy-tale land like Arabia. Hans Christian visited Arabia every night when his father read to him from *A Thousand and One Nights*. Hans Andersen was such a good reader that he made the adventures of Aladdin and Sindbad seem real. He also read plays to Hans Christian. Sometimes they acted them out with the puppet theater that Hans Andersen had made for his son.

The puppet theater was Hans Christian's favorite toy. He had seven puppets—a king and a queen, a jester, a beggar, and some soldiers. They fought battles, fell in love, and found fame and fortune, just like characters in stories his father read aloud.

When Hans Christian was six years old, his mother dressed him in his best clothes. It was time for him to go to school. Anne Marie never learned to read and wanted to be sure her son knew how.

Hans Andersen wanted his son to have a proper education so he could get ahead in the world and be more than a shoemaker.

School, for Hans Christian, was a room in a small house at the end of a narrow street. The teacher, an old woman, sat in a high-backed chair at the front of the class and taught the children their lessons. When Anne Marie saw a cane hanging on the wall beside the woman, she said her son must never be hit. Hans Christian was a gentle, well-behaved child, she insisted.

At first, Hans Christian *was* well behaved. There were mostly girls in the class, and he got along well with them. He learned his letters and began to read simple stories. But his favorite part of school was watching the grandfather clock at the front of the room. When the hour struck, a door opened in the clock's face, and two tiny figures danced into view.

One day while he was watching the figures twirl around and then dance back inside the clock, Hans Christian forgot about saying his lesson out loud with the rest of the class. Whack! All of a sudden, the teacher hit his knuckles with the cane. No adult had ever struck Hans Christian. He was shocked and scared. Without saying a word, he picked up his primer and ran home.

Anne Marie was surprised to see Hans Christian home so early, but when she heard his story, she didn't make him go back. Instead, she found a place for him in another school. Hans Christian was the youngest boy there, and the teacher held his hand at recess so he wouldn't be knocked down by the older boys. He soon became the teacher's pet, because he never got into fights and didn't misbehave in class. But even if he was the teacher's favorite, Hans Christian didn't learn much. He was a daydreamer, and school bored him.

While school didn't excite Hans Christian, the theater did. When he was seven years old, his parents took him to the theater for the first time. All through the play, he sat totally enchanted with the performance. The actors sang, they danced, and they talked to each other. It was like watching puppets come to life.

Much as he loved his puppet theater, Hans Christian knew at once that he loved *real* theater even more. The theater became his favorite place. His parents couldn't afford to buy tickets more than once a year, but Hans Christian made friends with the man who was in charge of the programs. In return for helping pass them out, Hans Christian could keep any left over. He took the programs home and made up entire plays for his puppet theater using the characters described on them.

Odense's theater sat on the main street near the homes of some of the wealthiest people in town. After school, Hans Christian often hung around the theater. He liked to watch the rich people promenade along the street in their fine clothes on their way to performances.

Would he ever wear anything but patched second-hand clothes, darned stockings, and wooden shoes? he wondered. Hans Christian was certain he would one day. After all, he told himself, wasn't life like a fairy tale?

When his grandmother told him stories, he was sure that his life would be special. She told Hans Christian that her own grandmother—his great-great-grandmother—had been a noble lady who wore beautiful clothes and lived in a fine house. But then she had fallen in love with a musician and married him against her parents' wishes. Ever since, the Andersen family had been poor.

The story wasn't really true, but it and his grandmother's other tales influenced Hans Christian greatly. Again and again, she told him how much better he was than the children he met at school and how much better his life was meant to be.

It seemed that life really was getting better when Hans Christian's father tried out for a job at a manor house in the country. He had to make a pair of shoes for a fine lady, and if they pleased her, Hans Andersen would become her family's shoemaker. The Andersens would live in a rent-free cottage with room for a garden and pasture for a cow.

Hans Christian's father worked hard to make the shoes perfect and was proud of the way they turned out. Everyone in his family agreed that they were beautiful and skillfully made. When he delivered them to the manor house, however, the lady took one look at the shoes and refused to try them on. They weren't to her taste at all. She angrily accused Hans Andersen of wasting her beautiful silk fabric. She would *never* wear such shoes! she said.

The Andersen family was crushed. Anne Marie had counted on doing the wash for the manor house while her family soaked up the sun and fresh country air. Hans Christian had dreamed about living next door to a house that was practically a castle. But Hans Andersen was the most disheartened.

For a while, he didn't know what to do with his life. Finally he decided to join the army. Denmark was an ally of France, whose army was waging war.

If he couldn't be a great lady's shoemaker, he would fight for his hero, Napoléon.

Hans Christian was eight years old when his father kissed him good-bye and went off to war. Sick in bed with measles, he sobbed as he listened to the beating drums that carried his father away. He had never been so sad, and he wondered if he'd ever see his father again.

② A Wonderful Voice

Two years later, Hans Andersen came home from war, much to his family's relief. Hans Christian could hardly wait to pull out his puppet theater and put on a play with his father. But Hans Andersen was too weak. His health had been ruined from marching many miles in cold and wet weather. He never fully recovered and died the following year.

When his father died, Hans Christian felt he had lost his best friend. He was lonelier than ever. His mother didn't have much time for him. He walked by himself most days to the city school for poor children, and most of the students left him alone. They thought he was odd, since he went around with his eyes closed, making up stories in his head. In his dreams, Hans Christian had friends and was always the hero. But whenever he told his stories to the other children, they laughed at him.

He got along much better with adults. His neighbors, the widow Mrs. Bunkeflod and her dead husband's sister, liked Hans Christian's stories so much that they let him borrow books from their library.

He soon discovered his favorite author: William Shakespeare, the great playwright. Hans Christian memorized long passages from the plays and recited them aloud for the old ladies. They clapped every time he performed for them.

He performed for other people too—whether they wanted to hear him or not. When he had written a play he thought was just like one of Shakespeare's, Hans Christian went up and down the street, from door to door, reading it aloud.

Not everyone thought the play was as wonderful as he did. Some people were alarmed by the sight of the tall, gawky boy acting out his play. They said he was becoming just like his grandfather. (Hans Christian's grandfather was insane but harmless. He roamed around town singing songs and wearing flowers in his hair.)

Other people told Anne Marie her son was too old—why, he was twelve!—to be doing nothing worthwhile. Many boys his age and younger were already learning a trade.

Anne Marie was earning barely enough money to support them, and a small amount from Hans Christian would certainly help. After talking to different tradesmen in Odense, she found a job for her son at a cloth mill. Hans Christian's grandmother thought it was terrible of Anne Marie to make him work with such common people. But he didn't mind being at the cloth mill. He told the other workers how well he could sing and dance, so they let him entertain them while they did his share of the work.

Then one day when Hans Christian sang in his highest and purest voice, some of the workers said he must be a girl. To Hans Christian's horror, they grabbed him by his arms and legs and tried to pull off his clothes. He finally tore himself loose and almost flew home. Anne Marie promised she'd never send him there again.

Hans Christian was thirteen years old and still without a job when his mother married another shoemaker. They all moved to a cottage next to the river. Hans Christian's new stepfather thought Anne Marie spoiled her son and couldn't understand why the boy didn't get a job. But Anne Marie told him her son wasn't ready to go to work yet.

Anne Marie herself still worked as a washer-woman, and Hans Christian still liked to go down to the river with her. A large boulder lay at the side of the river. While Anne Marie used the rock to put out her wash, Hans Christian pretended it was a stage. He stood at the top and sang songs he made up as he went along. Hans Christian's mother and the other washerwomen weren't the only people to hear his songs. A rich gentleman lived on the other side of a wooden fence near the boulder. Some summer evenings, he brought visitors into his garden. Whenever Hans Christian knew they were there, he sang in his finest voice.

People began sending for him to come to their homes and sing. Before long, Prince Christian of Odense had heard about the poor boy who had such a wonderful voice. He invited Hans Christian to come to his castle to perform.

In daydreams, Hans Christian had pretended he lived in a castle, and now his dream had nearly come true, at least for a short time. He was dazzled by the castle. As he stood before Prince Christian in a long room, he sang his best songs. Smiling, the prince clapped after each one. Encouraged by the prince's warm response, Hans Christian raced through some of the plays he had memorized.

When he stopped for breath, the prince asked him what his future plans were.

To be an actor, Hans Christian answered. More than anything in the world, he wanted to be an actor.

Prince Christian pointed out that although Hans Christian's performance was good, he was poor. He'd be better off learning a trade. Wouldn't he like to be a wood turner, a tailor, or a clerk? Perhaps the prince could help him get an apprenticeship.

No, Hans Christian replied, he wanted only to work in the Royal Theater in Copenhagen. Anne Marie also tried to persuade her son to learn a trade. (She thought he would make a good tailor, because he had so much practice sewing clothes for his puppets.) But Hans Christian reminded her of his father's words: "No matter what the boy wants to do, even if it's the silliest thing in the world, let him have his way."

Anne Marie insisted he was too young to go to Denmark's capital. He didn't know a single person there. What would he *do* in Copenhagen? she asked.

"I will become famous!" he told her. "First you go through terrible suffering, and then you become famous."

Anne Marie tried to reason with him. He didn't have enough money, she said, and she couldn't send him any. But Hans Christian had a ready answer. He took out the piggy bank that held all the money he had ever earned—from singing, running errands, and coins people had given him. He smashed the clay pig and counted thirteen rigsdaler, enough to live on for a few weeks.

Anne Marie was running out of arguments. Finally she took her son to an old wisewoman who told fortunes. Maybe the old woman could talk some sense into Hans Christian, Anne Marie reasoned. But maybe, Hans Christian thought, the old woman would tell him of his fairy-tale life to come.

After consulting her cards, the woman said, "Your son will become a great man, and to his honor Odense shall be illuminated one day." The wisewoman told Hans Christian something he already believed—he was destined to become famous. Someday candles would light up every window in Odense, just for him.

③

A Place in the Theater

Hans Christian Andersen arrived in Copenhagen on September 6, 1819, eager to become famous. It was a glorious day. The water in the blue sound separating Denmark and Sweden sparkled in the morning sun. Pale green copper spires and splendid towers rose above the city walls. As Hans Christian stood before one of the four great gates set in the green ramparts that protected the city, he was overcome by emotion. It was like a fairy kingdom. He burst into tears at the beautiful sight.

Before long, however, he dried his eyes and rented a cheap room at an inn just inside one of the city gates. Then he headed straight for the Royal Theater. Walking around the building again and again, he prayed to God to make him an actor. When a ticket seller offered him a ticket to the next performance, Hans Christian could not believe his luck. He thanked the man and put the ticket in his pocket, not realizing he had to pay money for it.

The man snatched it back, called him a gawky, good-for-nothing boy, and told him to go away.

Frightened, Hans Christian ran all the way back to the inn and had a good cry. When he recovered, he thought again about how he was going to find work. Before he left Odense, he had begged Iversen, one of the town's leading citizens, for a letter of introduction to Madame Schall. She was the most famous dancer at the Royal Theater. To Hans Christian, she seemed like a fairy queen, and fairy queens granted worthy people their wishes. Having no doubt that he was a worthy person, he prayed that she would get him a job.

The next morning Hans Christian dressed carefully in his only suit and put on a hat so big it nearly covered his eyes. It was early when he arrived at Madame Schall's home, and he waited several hours for her to get up. As soon as she awoke, her servant told her all about the strange-looking boy who was sitting in her parlor. Finally she agreed to see him, even though she had never heard of Hans Christian Andersen or of Iversen.

Hans Christian wanted to become an actor so badly that he didn't waste a minute of Madame Schall's time. To prove he had talent, he offered at once to act out the role of Cinderella.

He had seen the play twice in Odense and had memorized every word. Taking off his hat and boots so he could dance more easily, Hans Christian sang and pranced around the room, using his hat as a tambourine.

At first Madame Schall was stunned, then she was shocked. Did he imagine for a moment that what he was doing was dancing? she asked. When the room began to shake from his great leaps, she stopped him. She didn't want the floor to collapse! She told him to get dressed and go away.

Hans Christian pulled on his boots while great tears rolled down his cheeks. Madame Schall couldn't help feeling sorry for him and said maybe he could eat at her house now and then. Hans Christian offered to run errands for her, but she didn't want an errand boy. She suggested he see one of the directors of the Royal Theater if he really wanted a job.

"Too thin for the theater." That's what the director said after looking Hans Christian up and down. Hans Christian replied that if the director would hire him with a good salary, "then I shall soon get fat!" But when the director said the theater only hired educated people, Hans Christian had no quick reply.

These rejections were discouraging, but Hans Christian didn't give up. There were a few coins left from his piggy bank, and he believed that miracles could happen. In the newspapers, he had read about an Italian, Giuseppe Siboni, who had been appointed director of the Royal Theater's singing school. Hans Christian decided to visit him.

When he rang the bell, Siboni's housekeeper answered. Her master was having a dinner party, she said, and couldn't see him. Hans Christian was so disappointed that he poured out the story of his life to her. He said Siboni was his last hope for a job in the theater, his last hope in all the world. The housekeeper told him to stay right where he was while she talked to her master.

Siboni and his guests came out of the dining room to inspect their visitor. They wondered how anyone who looked so odd could have any talent. His clothes were shabby and ill fitting, and his big hands and feet kept getting in the way of each other. But Siboni decided to give him a chance. He led the boy to the piano and asked him to sing.

Hans Christian's high, clear voice filled the room, and everyone clapped. Then to show that he could do more than sing, he acted out two scenes from a play and recited some poems. The poems were so sad that Hans Christian's true feelings broke through, and he burst into tears. Instead of laughing at him, Siboni and his guests said he had genuine talent and would almost certainly find work in the Royal Theater.

But first his voice had to be trained, and Siboni offered to give him singing lessons, free of charge. He would also provide meals for him every day at his home. Siboni's guests even took up a collection so Hans Christian could pay his rent for the next few months.

Everything went well until spring, when he turned fifteen. It had been a cold, wet winter, and Hans Christian had no umbrella or galoshes. Each day he walked through ice and slush to get to Siboni's, and the soles of his shoes had holes in them. He caught many colds and often couldn't sing. Worse still, his voice began to change.

Because he was changing from boy to man, Hans Christian's lovely soprano voice was soon gone forever. Siboni said he was sorry, but he could no longer keep him in his singing school. He also told Hans Christian he was too tall, too thin, and too awkward for the theater. Furthermore, theater patrons expected educated performers. Why not return to Odense and learn a trade? Siboni asked.

These were harsh words, and Siboni was a trusted friend, but Hans Christian could not imagine a life for himself outside the theater. He racked his brains until he thought about ballet. Ballet required neither education nor a good voice. And not all ballet dancers were great beauties. Hans Christian's friends put in a good word for him, and Dahlén, the head of the Royal Theater's dancing school, agreed to let him attend classes on a trial basis.

When Dahlén gave Hans Christian a small part in a ballet as a giant troll, he was thrilled. Even better, his name appeared in the program as a member of the cast: "TROLL—ANDERSEN." It was the first time he had seen his name in print, and Hans Christian was so excited that he carried the program wherever he went. He even took it to bed with him at night, reading his name over and over by candlelight.

For a moment, it seemed that his dreams were coming true. But at the end of the spring season, he was dismissed from the theater. Dahlén told him he simply wasn't graceful enough for ballet. He would never become more than an extra.

Hans Christian was stunned. After three years in Copenhagen, he was back where he had started.

But he refused to give up his dream. There had to be a place for him in the theater. Singing, dancing, and acting hadn't brought success, but perhaps he could write a play.

The first play Hans Christian submitted to the Royal Theater was rejected immediately. Such bad grammar! Such horrible spelling! the directors said. Hans Christian knew he could do better. He wrote a second play, which he read to anyone who would listen. People liked it so well that he was sure the Royal Theater would want the play. With high hopes, he delivered it to the directors.

Then he waited and waited. Hans Christian waited all summer for a reply. Soon he was desperately short of money and often had nothing to eat. He also needed new clothes. He had outgrown his old ones and never stood up straight because everything was too short. His bony wrists hung far below the ends of his sleeves, and his skinny legs stuck out beneath the bottom of his pants.

At last he heard from the directors of the Royal Theater. They would not put on his play, but they said there was a lot worthwhile in what Hans Christian had written. If he could get an education, they said, someday he might produce something worthy of being acted on the Danish stage.

Here was that word again: *education*. Everyone seemed to be telling him to get an education—the first person he had talked to at the Royal Theater, Siboni saying theater patrons expected educated performers, and now the theater's directors.

As much as Hans Christian hated the idea, getting an education seemed the only way to go. But how could he go back to school? He was seventeen years old. Most boys his age were leaving school. Where would he get the money?

The directors had the answer. They offered to arrange for his education. Jonas Collin, one of the most influential directors, recommended Hans Christian to King Frederik VI. The king granted him enough money to live on for three years, as well as free instruction in a boarding school at Slagelse, a small town about fifty miles from Copenhagen.

Hans Christian could not believe his luck. School wasn't his first choice, but what a relief not to have to worry about money for the next few years. He would have enough to eat and would be given clothes that fit him and shoes that kept the water out. And maybe there was something to be gained by becoming educated, Hans Christian thought. He had tried everything else.

④

Back to School

On a beautiful autumn day in 1822, Hans Christian set off on the mail coach for Slagelse. The town was small, with two churches, a windmill, a few streets of houses with red-tile roofs, and a copper tower or two. Jonas Collin had arranged for Hans Christian to stay with a kind widow. His bright room looked out onto a garden and rolling green fields beyond town. It was very different from the cheap cubbyholes he had rented in Copenhagen.

Two days after he arrived, Hans Christian enrolled in school. Although he was seventeen, he was placed in a class with twelve- and thirteen-year-old boys. He was nearly twice as tall as the other students and knew half as much.

They solved math problems quicker and could spell better. Spelling was especially hard for Hans Christian. He never seemed to spell a word the same way twice. Teachers nowadays would probably think he was dyslexic. But in the 1800s, people understood little about reading disabilities.

In spite of his difficulties, Hans Christian had the greatest desire to learn, and he worked hard. He studied long hours after school and struggled to catch up. His teachers were generally kind to him because he tried so hard. Still, they were amazed at his ignorance. The other boys were kind to him too because he was so friendly.

The headmaster, or principal, was a different story. Simon Meisling was short, fat, and easily irritated. Even though he worked with young people, he didn't understand them or their high spirits. All the boys in the school were afraid of him and did their best not to make him angry. His fiery temper matched his fiery red hair.

Everything Hans Christian did seemed to arouse Meisling's temper. No matter how well he knew his lessons, whenever Meisling called on him to recite, Hans Christian became so nervous that his mind would go blank. Or else he would stumble over his words and get everything mixed up.

Meisling took great delight in humiliating him. Whenever he came up with a wrong answer, Meisling bellowed that he had never seen anyone so stupid. Hans Christian's feelings were easily hurt, and he usually ended up in tears. Then Meisling ridiculed him for being such a crybaby.

Hans Christian was afraid of Meisling, but he was even more afraid of disappointing the friends in Copenhagen who had provided for his education. He wrote Jonas Collin about his fears—fear of failure and fear of Simon Meisling. Maybe he really was the good-for-nothing that Meisling said he was. Perhaps he should go to America, where in those days failures went to begin a new life.

Jonas wrote back that Hans Christian was not a failure. As long as he was studying and getting good marks, that's what mattered. Hans Christian felt a little better, but he longed for happier days.

He longed as well for a chance to write. Meisling had forbidden him to write any poetry or plays while he was in his school. Jonas Collin also told him not to spend time writing when he had so much schoolwork to do. But Hans Christian had so many feelings inside him that he just had to let them out. Late at night after his lessons were done, he wrote poems in secret.

On Sundays, Hans Christian stuffed his poems in his pockets and walked to the town of Soro, seven miles away. The poet Ingemann taught high school there. Two of his students wrote poetry, and they asked Hans Christian if he'd like to hear what they had written. They wanted to hear his poems, too.

Hans Christian did well enough in Meisling's school to be promoted to the third class when he was eighteen years old. Three more class years and he would graduate! Rather than go away during summer vacation, he stayed in Slagelse and read books. By the new term in 1825, he was one of the best in his class. The other boys asked him to write compositions for them but said not to make them so good that Meisling would realize they hadn't written them.

Even Meisling became friendly with him. At last Hans Christian thought he had won the headmaster's goodwill. But Meisling had a reason for being nice to him. Meisling *said* he wanted Hans Christian to live in his home as a member of his family. What he *really* wanted was the money Hans Christian paid his landlady each month. Furthermore, Mrs. Meisling planned to use Hans Christian as a baby-sitter for the three Meisling children.

Meisling suggested that Hans Christian write Jonas Collin to ask his permission to move. Meisling wrote Collin too, saying what a hard worker Hans Christian was and how much progress he had made. When Hans Christian found out what Meisling had said about him, he was extremely flattered.

But once Hans Christian moved into his home, Meisling began to bully him once more. Now there was no escape from his taunts. Whether at home or at school, Meisling made Hans Christian feel like a failure. He wondered if he should forget about school altogether.

Before Hans Christian gave up, he had a stroke of luck. Word got back to Jonas Collin that Meisling was treating Hans Christian horribly. As soon as Collin knew how bad things were, he had Hans Christian move back to Copenhagen. Collin provided him with a private tutor named Ludvig Müller. Müller, only a year older than Hans Christian, was gentle, kind, and encouraging—a wonderful change from Simon Meisling! He also worked tirelessly to prepare Hans Christian to pass the university exams.

Twice a day, Hans Christian walked across town to Müller's house. On the way there, he went over his lessons in his mind. But on his walk back home, his writer's eyes and ears took over. He noticed everything that was happening around him—the people hustling through the streets, the activity along the canal, the windmills turning on the grassy banks of the ramparts.

What a pity, he thought, that he had no time to write it all down. But with the exams scheduled for October, studying was more important. As the time approached, Hans Christian grew despondent. What if he didn't pass? What would all the people who had helped him think of him? On the day of the exams, he was so nervous that he fainted. Then he got a nosebleed. Much to his relief, he recovered and passed the exams. He was twenty-three years old and could go to the university. Better still, he hadn't let anyone down.

(5)

Love, Travel, and a Few Fairy Tales

Hans Christian was now considered an educated man. If he wanted, he could study to become a doctor, lawyer, or pastor. But in his heart, he wanted only to be a writer. When he asked Jonas Collin what he should do, Collin told him writing was also an honorable career. "Go in God's name along the road you seem fitted to take; that will probably be best for you," Collin told him.

All the words and ideas that Hans Christian had kept in his head flew "like a swarm of bees" into his first book. Published in 1829, *A Walking Tour from Holmens Canal to the Eastern Point of Amager* was filled with Hans Christian's humorous observations of what he had seen and heard on his walks across the canals to Müller's house. He enchanted his readers with sights and sounds they had strolled past without noticing. The book was an instant success.

Next, Hans Christian sat down and in eight days wrote a play, *Love in St. Nicholai Church Tower.* The Royal Theater accepted it for production that April. Many of Hans Christian's fellow students were in the theater on opening night. They clapped their approval and shouted, "Long live Andersen!" Hans Christian was so happy, tears filled his eyes.

Proud of his success, Hans Christian toured Odense in the summer. He hadn't seen his mother for four years and was shocked to see how old she had grown. Her bones ached, Anne Marie told her son, from standing all day in cold water and scrubbing other people's clothes. To lessen the pain and to warm herself up, she drank brandy. Now people said Anne Marie was an alcoholic. Hans Christian helped her as much as he could, remembering how well she had cared for him as a child.

He visited his mother again the next summer, then traveled to southern Fyn to visit a student friend, Christian Voigt. When Hans Christian met Voigt's sister Riborg, he fell in love for the first time. Riborg wasn't beautiful, but Hans Christian liked the way her brown eyes lit up when she laughed. She made him feel good because she knew his poetry and appreciated his writing. They took walks in the garden, and he wrote poems for her.

Riborg was unofficially engaged to her childhood sweetheart, but her parents didn't approve of the young man. Hans Christian thought he might have a chance to win her love.

As soon as he returned to Copenhagen, he wrote a letter asking if she was sure she loved her fiancé. If not, he said he would do anything necessary to make himself acceptable to her parents. Riborg wrote back that she couldn't make her childhood sweetheart unhappy. She believed it was her duty to remain faithful to him.

Hans Christian's heart was broken. To overcome his grief, he did what a lot of poets do: he wrote about his feelings in poem after poem. He also wrote a play about his love for Riborg called *To Meet and to Part*. (Unlike the outcome of his first love, the play had a happy ending.)

While critics had praised his earlier writings, now they didn't like anything he wrote. They talked about his careless grammar and bad spelling. Hans Christian defended himself by saying what mattered in poetry was the expression of feelings, not how the words were spelled. Other critics went back to his earlier works and pointed out all the grammatical errors. Some people read his poems only to find—and laugh at—all the mistakes.

Hans Christian's emotions exploded after all this criticism. He *would* become a poet whom they should honor, he told himself. His name *would* become famous throughout the world, just wait and see! Hans Christian felt as if everyone in Copenhagen was laughing at him. To make matters worse, his heart was still broken.

Edvard Collin, only a few years younger than Hans Christian, saw how his friend was suffering. Edvard suggested that the young writer use some of the money he had earned to travel. He might see some interesting sights. In any case, he would be out of Denmark when Riborg married.

In 1831, Hans Christian left on a six-week trip to Germany. He saw mountains for the first time, great Gothic cathedrals, and wonderful castles. In every town he visited, he met German writers. He also heard about two brothers, named Grimm, who were collecting folk myths and fairy tales.

When he returned to Denmark, he was still brokenhearted but not too unhappy to write a quick book about his travels. He hoped the critics would be kinder to him now, but he was disappointed. The critics wondered how anyone who had been in a country only six weeks could know enough to write a book about the place.

The critics had a point. Hans Christian was writing too many things too quickly. Good writers must revise what they write and often set their work aside for a while. Then when they reread it, they see how it can be improved.

But writing was the only way Hans Christian knew how to earn the money he needed for food, rent, and clothes. He didn't have time to revise and polish his work.

For a time, he grew very depressed. He needed a friend to talk to, a good listener. Hans Christian found that friend in the Collin household. When Louise, the youngest of the Collin children, was a child, Hans Christian had entertained her with a thousand amusing stories he made up. Now she was eighteen years old and listened sympathetically to his problems. Every time another person criticized his writing, Hans Christian poured out his heart to her.

Then a strange sensation came over him. He had had this feeling before. Was he in love? he wondered. Hans Christian did the only thing he knew to express his feelings for Louise: he wrote a poem about her beautiful blue eyes. When the Collin family went to their summer home in the country for a few months, he wrote daily letters and poems to her. He even wrote out the story of his life for her and stitched the pages together himself to make a book.

Louise thought of Hans Christian only as a brother. She was already falling in love with a young lawyer. When her engagement was announced on New Year's Day of 1833, Hans Christian was very hurt. He wanted to get away from everything—the critics, Louise and her fiancé, and Copenhagen. He didn't think of life as a fairy tale any longer, and he wondered if there would ever be a happy ending for him.

Edvard and Jonas helped Hans Christian apply for a two-year travel grant given by the Danish government to promising young artists. On April 22, 1833, the entire Collin family was at the boat to wish Hans Christian a good trip. While he said his good-byes, he prayed that he would either produce some important works that would make his friends proud to know him or die far away from Denmark.

Over the next several months, Hans Christian visited Germany, France, Switzerland, and Italy. Italy was the high point of his trip. The brokenhearted writer fell in love with the country. As he traveled around, he took in all the sights, sounds, and smells. In his diary, he commented on his travels and made more than a hundred sketches of scenes that charmed him and of people in their everyday lives.

He also began to write a novel, *The Improvisatore*. Set in Italy, the story is a disguised version of Hans Christian's life. The hero, Antonio, is a poor boy who makes up poems for people in the town marketplace. A nobleman recognizes his talent and gives him an education. Antonio then becomes a famous poet. The rest of the characters are people who were part of Hans Christian's life—his poor mother, his insane grandfather, the hateful headmaster Meisling, the kind Collin family—all disguised as Italians.

During his stay in Italy, Anne Marie died. Hans Christian had faithfully written to his mother while he was away and sent what money he could. Now he felt as if he were all alone in the world. But the feeling didn't last. When Hans Christian returned to Copenhagen, the Collin family greeted him as if their very own son had returned from a long trip. His love for Louise had faded, and he was able to meet her as a friend.

The first thing Hans Christian did when he got back was finish his novel. Edvard helped him catch misspellings and other mistakes. Hans Christian was so grateful for all that the Collins had done for him that he dedicated his novel to them. The front of the book reads: "To the Conference Counselor Collin and his noble wife, in whom I found parents, whose children were my brothers and sisters, whose house was my home, I present the best that I possess."

While he waited for his novel to come back from the printer, Hans Christian needed to pay rent, buy decent clothes, and repair the holes in his boots. So he wrote a pamphlet of four fairy tales. He called these tales "trifles," because he didn't consider them important. But he enjoyed writing them, and they brought in a small sum of much-needed money.

Hans Christian was almost thirty years old and had tried many forms of writing: poetry, plays, travel books, a novel, and now fairy tales. He didn't expect more than a few rigsdalers for the fairy tales, but he hoped his novels and plays would bring him both money and fame. Ever since he was a child, he had been sure he was destined to become famous. He wished it would happen soon.

⑥

Fame

The Improvisatore did well. Danish critics liked the book, and the novel became a great popular success. Bookstores couldn't keep enough copies on their shelves. Hans Christian was overwhelmed with joy at his novel's success.

The pamphlet of fairy tales got mixed reviews. One critic said, "It's not writing, it's talking." Hans Christian wrote the way people talked, and that kind of language had never been used before in Danish literature. Another critic said Hans Christian should not waste his time writing fairy tales for children. His tales were too much fun and would not improve children's minds. (In those days, people thought children had to learn something when they read.)

A few critics, however, thought the tales were the best things Hans Christian had ever written. They were even better than *The Improvisatore,* they said, and would make him famous. But Hans Christian only laughed at that idea. He was sure he would be remembered as the author of *The Improvisatore,* and he didn't write another fairy tale for a year. Instead, he finished his second novel and started a third. Then an idea came to him for a new story, and he couldn't resist writing it down. This tale, "The Little Mermaid," became one of his best known. He published it in a pamphlet of fairy tales that also included "The Emperor's New Clothes."

When Hans Christian wrote his first fairy tales, he thought they weren't important. But children loved them because they were told in words they could understand. The new style of written language made his stories easy for children to read and fun to read aloud. Older people liked them too.

Shop clerks recognized Hans Christian as the man who wrote "those tales," which pleased him very much. People pointed him out as he walked down the streets of Copenhagen, swinging his long arms and trying to manage his big feet. Strangers came up to him and told him how much they enjoyed his stories. They begged for more.

Why were Hans Christian's fairy tales so popular? Other fairy tales had been published, but Hans Christian's were different. The Grimm brothers traveled all around Germany in the early 1800s, collecting folk myths and fairy tales. They wrote down the stories exactly the way they heard them. When the Grimm brothers wrote their version of the folktale "The Tinderbox," for example, they began:

Once upon a time, there was a soldier who had served the king faithfully for many years. Now that the war was over and the soldier had been wounded many times, he could not serve any longer.

When Hans Christian retold the same tale, he jumped right into the story. The story begins:

A soldier came marching down the road: Left...right! Left...right! He had a pack on his back and a sword at his side. He had been in the war and he was on his way home. Along the road he met a witch. She was a disgusting sight, with a lower lip that hung all the way down to her chest.

Hans Christian's first fairy tales were retellings of tales he had heard in his childhood. But as he continued to write, he looked for story ideas in different places. He had been making up stories ever since he was a child, and he never ran out of ideas. He invented stories about common things such as tin soldiers, teapots, furniture, and vegetables—and he made them come alive. After a tree is cut down and used as a family Christmas tree in the story "The Fir Tree," it gets a "bark-ache" from its heavy ornaments.

Hans Christian saw stories everywhere. He wrote, "Often it seems to me that every fence, every little flower said 'Just look at me, then you'll know my story!'" One time a friend kidded Hans Christian, saying he could write about anything, even a darning needle. Hans Christian went straight up to his room, thought about how a darning needle might talk, and wrote:

"I have lived in a box belonging to a lady," began the darning needle. "She was a cook, and she had five fingers on each hand. There never existed creatures so conceited as those fingers; and yet they were only there to take me out of the box and put me back..."

"The Darning Needle" soon became known as one of his most humorous tales.

Many of Hans Christian's tales came from his personal experience. He remembered feeling different from everyone else, and he wrote about it in "The Little Mermaid" and "The Ugly Duckling." He never forgot how he had trembled with fear when the bullies chased him, and many of his fairy-tale characters feel fear. He knew how it felt to be poor and cold and hungry, so in "The Little Match Girl," he wrote about a girl desperate to sell matches for food and shelter.

The typical fairy tale ends with "...and they lived happily ever after." Hans Christian's stories don't always have happy endings. When the little match girl burns up all her matches for warmth, she freezes to death during the night. When the little mermaid falls in love with the prince, she gives up her beautiful voice so the sea witch will make her look like a human being. When she can't speak to the prince about her love for him, he marries someone else.

Unlike the unhappy endings of many of his fairy tales, Hans Christian's life began to be filled with happy times. Royal families invited him to their castles and palaces. Friends asked him to stay in their country homes and treated him like a prince.

In the evenings after dinner, everyone looked forward to hearing his latest fairy tales, which he still read to anyone who would listen.

Reading them aloud helped him learn what was good about the tales and what didn't work. Then he could revise his stories and make them better. Hans Christian still wrote quickly, but he had come to realize how much better his stories were when he took the time to rewrite them.

Even though Hans Christian had become famous for his fairy tales, it bothered him that the critics only thought of him as a writer for children. He created his tales for both adults and children. "I seize on an idea for older people," he wrote, "and then tell it to the young ones, while remembering that father and mother are listening and must have something to think about."

Hans Christian was successful, but he wasn't completely happy. He longed to marry and have a home of his own. When he was thirty-eight years old, he fell in love for the last time. Jenny Lind was a young opera singer from Sweden. Although she wasn't pretty, her beautiful voice made her seem so. Everyone called her the Swedish Nightingale. Like Hans Christian, she had come from a poor family, was deeply emotional, and loved the theater.

When she came to Copenhagen to sing, he sent her poems and flowers every day. He wanted to ask her to marry him but didn't have the courage. On the day her ship left to return to Sweden, he gave her a letter declaring his love. Although she was fond of him, Jenny couldn't love him back. She wanted to be his friend, not his wife.

Hans Christian had lost at love again. This time, instead of taking a long trip to get over his disappointment, he stayed home and poured his emotions into a new fairy tale called "The Nightingale." In the tale, the emperor of China hears a common gray bird sing the most beautiful song he has ever heard. (The bird, a nightingale, represents Jenny Lind.) The emperor invites the nightingale to sing in his palace and tries to keep the bird in a cage.

Then one day the emperor receives a gift—a mechanical singing bird. The bird is covered with rubies, gold, and diamonds and is so beautiful to look at that the emperor doesn't mind that it can sing only one song. While the emperor and his court are admiring the mechanical bird, the nightingale flies away.

Later, when the music box wears out and the mechanical bird can no longer sing, the emperor is so sad he almost dies. The nightingale flies to a tree branch outside the palace window and sings until the emperor gets well. Then the nightingale promises to sing for the emperor whenever he likes, as long as it can remain free.

Hans Christian thought of his own nightingale, Jenny. Children and others read the story without knowing all its meaning but loved it just the same.

His fairy tales brought him more fame as the years went by. Hans Christian realized he was a national hero when his hometown of Odense invited him to a celebration in his honor. On December 6, 1867, city hall was decorated with banners, and red and white flags flew from every house. Schools were closed, and children joined the rest of the people crowding the streets to welcome him.

That night a candle burned in every window of every house. The old wisewoman's prophecy had come true. Odense was illuminated in honor of Hans Christian Andersen. He wished that his mother, father, and grandmother could have been there. Nearly fifty years had passed since he had told Anne Marie, ''First you go through terrible suffering, and then you become famous.''

Afterword

Hans Christian Andersen continued to write fairy tales, even in his old age. Nearly every year around Christmas, another slim volume of tales was published. His stories were known around the world and were translated into many languages. He became Denmark's most famous writer.

Although Hans Christian never had a family or home of his own, his many friends looked after him. In 1874, some of these friends raised money to put up a monument in his honor. The statue is larger than life and shows him looking down at his viewers with a book in his hands. Today, Danes as well as visitors to Copenhagen go to the King's Gardens, a public park, to see their beloved Hans Christian Andersen. He seems to be still reading his tales aloud to anyone who will listen.

Hans Christian lived to be seventy years old. He was ill the last two years of his life and wrote no more tales. On August 4, 1875, he died. All the bells in the city rang during the funeral march through the streets of Copenhagen. Thousands of mourners, young and old, crammed into the cathedral to pay their last respects, and for days afterward, crowds surrounded his grave. To this day, his grave is never without flowers.

Booklist

Stories and Fairy Tales by Hans Christian Andersen

The Complete Fairy Tales and Stories. Translated by Erik
Christian Haugaard. New York: Doubleday, 1974.
Seven Tales. Translated by Eve Le Gallienne. Illustrated
by Maurice Sendak. New York: Harper & Row, Publishers, 1959.

Selected Tales, Retold and Adapted

The Cowboy and the Black-Eyed Pea. Adapted from
"The Princess on the Pea" by Tony Johnston. Illus-
trated by Warren Ludwig. New York: G. P. Putnam's
Sons, 1992.
Once Upon a Princess and a Pea. Adapted from "The
Princess on the Pea" by Ann Campbell. Illustrated by
Kathy Osborn Young. New York: Stewart, Tabori &
Chang, 1993.
The Principal's New Clothes. Adapted from "The Em-
peror's New Clothes" by Stephanie Calmenson. New
York: Scholastic, Inc., 1989.
The Steadfast Tin Soldier. Adapted by Tor Seidler. Illus-
trated by Fred Marcellino. New York: HarperCollins/di
Capua, 1992.
The Tinderbox. Adapted and illustrated by Barry Moser.
Boston: Little, Brown & Co., 1990.
The Wild Swans. Adapted by Deborah Hautzig. Illus-
trated by Kaarina Kaila. New York: Alfred A. Knopf,
1992.

Bibliography

Andersen, Hans Christian. *The Complete Fairy Tales and Stories*. Translated by Erik Christian Haugaard. New York: Doubleday, 1974.

Andersen, Hans Christian. *The Fairy Tale of My Life: An Autobiography*. New York: Paddington Press, 1975.

Andersen, Hans Christian. *The True Story of My Life*. Translated by Mary Howitt. New York: The American-Scandinavian Foundation, 1926.

Arden, Harvey. "The Magic World of Hans Christian Andersen." *National Geographic* 156 (December 1979).

Böök, Fredrik. *Hans Christian Andersen: A Biography*. Norman, OK: University of Oklahoma Press, 1962.

Burnett, Constance Buel. *The Shoemaker's Son: The Life of Hans Christian Andersen*. New York: Random House, 1941.

Godden, Rumer. *Hans Christian Andersen: A Great Life in Brief*. New York: Alfred A. Knopf, 1965.

Grønbech, Bo. *Hans Christian Andersen*. Boston: Twayne Publishers, 1980.

Moore, Eva. *The Fairy Tale Life of Hans Christian Andersen*. New York: Scholastic, Inc., 1969.

Stirling, Monica. *The Life and Times of Hans Christian Andersen*. London: Collins, 1965.

Toksvig, Signe. *The Life of Hans Christian Andersen*. London: Macmillan and Co., Ltd., 1933.